ALSO BY C.E. PUTNAM

POETRY

The Papier-Mâché Taj Mahal
Spaces Where Spaces Are
Transmissions from the Institute
Maniac Box
Things Keep Happening

COLLABORATIONS

Crawlspace
  with Daniel Comiskey
Did You Ever Hear of a Think Like That?
  with Robb Putnam (images / sculpture)
XX Elegies
  with John Donne
Communal Bebop Canto
  with Allison Cobb and Jen Coleman

THE BIRD MAY BE DEAD BUT IT IS YOUR BIRD

POEMS BY

C.E. PUTNAM

P.I.S.O.R. PUBLICATIONS ✪ PORTLAND, OREGON

Cover photographs by the author

Thanks to the editors and curators where some of these poems first appeared: Lindsay Ruoff (*1001: A Literary Journal*), dan raphael (*Talking Earth-KBOO FM*), Paul Nelson (*Make it True: Poetry from Cascadia*), Richard Roundy (*Across the Margin*), David Kirschenbaum (*Boog Lit*), Gina Myers & Gabriella Torres (*The Tiny*), Lindsey Boldt & Steve Orth (*Where Eagles Dare*). Great gratitude to my readers Ethan Fugate, Jen Coleman and Susan Landers for their insight, support, and inspiration.

ISBN: 978-1-965345-00-9

P.I.S.O.R. Publications
Putnam Institute for Space Opera Research
Portland, Oregon
https://www.pisor-industries.org

Contents

To Nic and Maureen

THE BIRD MAY BE DEAD BUT IT IS YOUR BIRD

The Fantastic Skimmer Is Likely to Be Encountered

Maybe it's because ducks
don't talk much
when they are flying.
Few have hearts so dark

and broken they will
not bother to look
up when they hear
the barking of wild

geese and think for a moment
that they are upside down
birds looking down
on themselves, barking.

I

The Relation Between You and You Makes You

The whole day today
floating in a kidney
shaped swimming pool
algae plumed and starred
with koi polished stones.

First, a bar of cloud.

Warm long grasses in the distance
churned up my arctic stomach breezes.

Then, floating on my back,
I counted the leaves
of an enormous fan palm
waving all-confounding
blue vulgar shadows and
watched silken pigeon droppings
coo and wink their way down
to the pink tiled bottom.

A caretaker frightened
away a gang of dive-bombing
crows with an empty blue
water cooler bottle.

Blue plastic black
feather loop smacking
loop.

Later, I pleased my imagination
with the idea of The First Circle,
a rusted ring without center
under which I always find
another wider, darker one
opening wrecked without
beginning or end and thinking
I will never-ever-ever forget
their order until I lost leaf
count and had to start over
alive and stupid with wonder.

Winding River: a Part I Could Not Borrow

Drop of water to drop of water
dragonfly-leisure and vagabond
buzz debt barging up river and down.
Thirty more years wearing flowered
shirts conversing with the bodies
they want. Add temporary works:
a knot of roots under a parking lot,
an egret in its egg wondering what
its wings are for. But who is going
to purchase that? Subtract phase rewards:
we must write all our animals now.
I revolve in the gravity of spirits above
the sea electric with Napoleon
below on that prison island beating
the air, flightless and stupid. Red
cranes spoil the beaches, and then
my isolation feels so mechanical.
I am following a single water bug's total
circuit from truck bed (10 PAX) to pink
funnel to yellow work boots. Lizards
in the stairwell, ants in the walls.
There is a deep, deep distance I feel it
out there, an internal ocean, tiding up
beyond any horizon. I need to see
our planet in the water, the white
flower does not stop going down.

The Everlasting Noodle Is Its Own Delight

It is not just a feeling
of corruption without profit
without you outside the city
walls inside the city walls
then some noodles taking off
shoes in our tiny days
bowling on red carpet
my dear fish balls someone
is howling three times
along with the cardboard
pile in the stairwell three
times the spicy broth
with peanuts is over there
look away three times not many
happy days filled to the brim
bean sprouts on top remember
when we took ourselves off
into the moonlit hangar
and were floating so high up
and beyond all stars we might
as well have that as our tender
keepsake falling away.

Clementi Meadows

From Sun Base Down, I think
I see worldwide chaos float above
the Sea Apple trees and land.
I'll just float through this life,
disordered. Mynah bird orchestra
as the opposite of a dream somehow
blames me. Deafened survivors normalize
their passenger miles from the accident
lacking radar. The moon is just a bat-ball
to bats. A trail of Old Yeller candlelight
traces the riverbank, singing. You keep
telling me but I still cannot see a towering
red cloud blooming in the west.
Nothing but goddamned flowers.

This Tree Is Easy to Climb

In no time at all the Smoke
Mangoes had been eaten.
I put a silver penny
in the music box.

A large Insect-O-Freak
antennae growing
through a fourth
floor window frame.

Midtown incinerators
blacken the new
fallen snow with Styrofoam ash.

Yowling hounds get kissy
after a second bowl
of mimosa. The yellow
orange flesh browns
and sours. I spit out
red plastic bags.
I want to eat a wolf
but I'm afraid this will change
me. A trail of roach
droppings now over my legs
how did I get this
paralyzed—twitching
a panicked creature bumping
against the lid of the boil pot
or lawn mowers running
loose in freshly buried caskets.

Does your belly bear
the mark of the six stars?

No one really knows
about my absolute hunger
since my diagnosis a small
sweet lick of the underbelly
can feed my music machine.

O, green tambourine
I just want to watch
my life go by undisturbed.

Country Vivid

With the all-new wild
runoff you can
now worry all
the time for less
in a country as yet
to be without
complex concrete
maze voids from
my sawed off chair
I don't know which:
the silver oil
drying into snakes
or the office
flower bridge
recrossing colorful
enriched sand dunes:
red cake yellow cake
it is too late to taste.
Gone off to be more selfless
tobacco in the coffee
shop air always seems so
optically thin I flip over
every blue table but never
find any living thing.

The Universe Is Growing Slower

Air quivering above
the red dirt road quickens
the day locusts' hissing
but I stay still and shaded
sweating out the rice whiskey,
smoked catfish, and red
spice rushing in my head.
I want you more now. Besides
who would want to steal
a psycho away from me?
Pouring out clot blood
to live in disgust: eat with it,
sleep with it. First vertebrates
are you listening to this?
Coffee rings bubbled onto
my face. I can smell you
making a king-sized
order of filth rice, fried
is the heart, the universe,
we are lying near its center
feeling a low idling hum wind
down. Should I go out into the night
alone to discover what it is?
Last light stealing to bleach out
you and your bed selfless,
lonesome plains, our desires
stiffened with yak hair.
We begin clean on a paper blanket
square to count the fading stars
circling bodies by the millions.

Goodness Will Be Decreasing While Evil Increases

I remember the field
by the red lantern seller
as it was before
the red lantern seller
ever was and for a moment
might imagine the way
suffering can be both your body
and a nest. Now, a fire engulfs
the field. And I study
the way a broken bird emerges
from the loosened earth and beaks
a horrid path in struggle
to get to light to be as amazing
as it may seem: a pale blue
egg again in afternoon sun.
Maybe after 2,112 transformations
I will also be flattened, glowing
polished silver, friend of all
the universe, friend to all I see.

The Acorn Helmet

The killers fogged
the everlasting pines—
roots torn / no sprout
survives it submerged
ghosts in a public fountain
filled with bleach
it was one way to
get to the afterlife.

I picked up the pinecone
in case someone else
might come along
and discover it
whenever I smell it
I am reminded of war.

Before the Autumn Ends

Before the autumn ends
my pant legs
rotted with filth
—season of withering
hoarfrost—my blood
crosses my heart
—why does it do that
to me it makes me this time
—sky at once—
and makes me die.
You call and call and
come by but you
never hear me
reply, but I am always
coming! Coming
down to open the door!
My friend I think
you are happy,
but I am wrong
you are really super sad
super sad just like me.

Facing Snow

Turned the state
news off to watch
the red furnace fire.
War cry louder
than a new ghost
fresh from the burn bed.

snow's back   wind wails

The abandoned gourd
scoop turns statue
green. Worry sits
empty in its soup.

low cloud   low dusk

Reading this book
without independent grief.

Plain Wilderness

Western mountain snow fall or ash
fall every city has three weather
garrisons buttressing against the ice
storm. Citizens gather on Goon
River's midnight ice clear watching
frozen drone pigeons fall from the bridge
roped off drunk and starlit. Inside
the shortwave Everly Brothers
separate Tanya's tears one by one,
saving the dark sick ones to cross
the horse out. Without you I had
to endure that song "Unbearable
Personal Day Depression" all by
my lonesome, all by myself.

Breakfasts Exert on Each Other
a Similar Occult Power

Inside the pre-dawn
eating house the waitress
preps the whisper
butter. Eavesdropping
I spread it around
all day quietly typing
letters at first then
reducing them down
to three or four words:
"this message is not
just to thank you for
your trailer order."
A report is one thing,
but believing it
contains something
more, is another.
Of course to explain
the new to people
who object to new
ideas, you must
abandon any hope
of a shared realization
and just wait for the skin
on the milk pudding
to set. What is left?
An unsteady hand
on a cocked pancake
gun, a slice of black
powder pie, a Hungarian

hangover desperate
for cream and sugar.
Look at the bees lying
dead along the grease
caked window sills. You
will find no difference
in their individual tiny
deaths at first. The cockroach
twitches towards its food,
the pollen bends to the bee,
an egg waits inside the belly
of the caterpillar until the eaten
becomes the eater again, just
as my corpse will be drawn
to its first corpse fly. I don't
think you can remove the egg
from the cell it attaches to. But
give it a spoon—while I double
check the vending chains
while whirling the air
with the commotion of illicit
gumball spending. The mosaic
virus mottles the leaf in your hand
with red and brown and stars.
But aren't those the same
stars what kept us down on
the earth for so long? A few
hours later high up in my room
looking down at world's end,
pockets filled with change
cold black coffee alone with you.

II

Why Should We Describe These Beautiful Trees?

Hello rude lines
take another pill

Why draw anything?
my eye can open any picture!

Overlord power ridiculous
as a treadmill making

cripples picturesque
pig nipples for lunch

Hello miraculous dots
let me be you forever

your accordion is beautiful
until it is played

I am running out
of infinitude whichever

direction I go The Frescoes
of Dan sparking cold spring

buds and separating smoky
heaven and dusty earth

the palm leaves please
all of the charm out of

algebra white flowers litter
saw buck heaven

the pine trees
condition of fire.

I Thought Spiders

I thought spiders building webs inside the goat's eye.
And that goat was my only way home.

Unhappily, a Small Room

that is your living
room and the living

room for a very large
family of beavers.

Covering every edge
a pile of leaves.

Each beaver rakes
to make a bed

of its own
gnaws the bark

suckles and rears
to make of the center

a dining room
a new world

between chin
and forepaws

refusing to adjust to
the conditions of the age.

Scheme of Motions

Before the Scheme of Motions
could belong to each

there was only a single
living substance

which all things now separate
into all-together opposites:

A duck egg appears
between the folds

the bubble wrap membranes
could no longer bear or hold

the much larger creature
growing inside them

summer light and cucumber trees
both in turn, turn inward.

A tucked beak—the unharvested
blooming inside of you

the three great departments
of the world.

Universal Kind of Abstract

I had been nothing
once because I lived

after my beheading
my knees felt bad

of course I can smash
rocks with my head

it is hard to stay in Hell
when I know it is a trick

the sky is playing on me
please let me go.

The Infinity of the Heavenly Seas

The tabernacle shape
of our nice universe

the dead waters were
above it the dying waters

were below that it is of
the earth that the water

should not be like that
orca blowhole gorged

and clogged with waste
to sail dreaded upon it

in a state of vapor to
never bring the world

back to its starting point
in the same limit of time.

And Under Them, the Nobody-Stars

They hid behind
the twinkle after
hearing my cry
for help bending
my right elbow
bringing down
my foot from
the shelf and boot
it. My foot
wants the pear
farmer. My foot
wants to scar
the farmer's heart
with a seed that
cannot make
another tree
make anything
at all.

The Sublime Totality

Non-toxic
skull flower
how do you
know my name?
Bone precisely
sealing wax
harmonizing watchful
hygiene in action
glass stoppers
an erogenous
center spinning
between twenty-one
and slaughter
the exhibitionist
is relaxed before
the magistrate
you will let this
understanding enter
you I am me
without me I
tell myself
I am the sock
of all creatures
no foot paw
or hoof can
exist without
me.

It Is Always Amusing to See You Eat Bread

But why would
the chicken wings

swing back like that
pulling the children

back into the planes
where they had previously

existed? So tell me,
when you press

that blue button on your
belt, your waist is pulled

in a direction
at a perfect right angle

to all the directions
you could possibly

go in outer space?
I don't believe you.

The button doesn't
even light up.

Deskbound Trees

I won't forget
and you should
remember too
that this is me
doing the best
that I can interplanetary
oh I know interplanetary
oh yes I know
   interplanetary
      interplanetary.
The Earth
what have you
remains fixed
a zenith marked
but planets
can orbit
on their own
outside me our child
the moon our fire
the sun and probably
everything else
all wasted or worse
under smoked glass
it is not an ending
how you break
the day that is
every day from
now on or just
fuck that for a little while
this graveyard geology

springtime haze
green maple leaves
and finally coming around
to appreciating
the planet Venus
because it gives us
another world
that we cannot live on
that is not Earth.

Sometimes in My Hands, a Package

Who deer the common gifts
dark green passing into night

the legend of a lamb lost
in the farmer's corn dead

the sky streams through purple
the afternoon I pretended

I invented the balloon
and am still wrecked

by not getting credit
for it instead of what I am

really wrecked about.

Welcome to Your Orientation

When I tell the tick
to stop drinking blood
and when it won't stop
I will have to lick it.
One must die
before the other.
I was expected to
complete all my work
over the weekend to re-total
the tabulations and sit
with them my heart
deep chest with my fist
drunk until I could not
keep my eyes open
tying the wire ends
together it felt great
getting shocked. I
fingered my puffed
ankle—it came up
through my other foot
I cannot afford another
interruption probably
my last chance.

Influence Worm

Give me your hand, at first look
you will think it is in the warts
but no, it begins inside you, slowly
moving through the tasseled
grass in your belly. Its voice sounds
like the language of facts, but soon
blooms wondrous wild blood flowers
and vines, a spiritual x-ray
taken from the inside. When held up
to the lightbox-sun you feel
(but cannot know) the sense of things
as things themselves, but that illumination
soon leaves your head-heart area,
the shadow losing contrast decays
and takes root in your retentive organs.
Soon the head, the heart, become senseless
and thus as the warts weaken, you lose your fear,
but gain a sickness, a solvent that destroys
you piecemeal with every tiny breath or swallow.

Money Devil

A money devil tried
to seduce me by strewing
gold coins about. It was
the sound that first caught
my attention, I thought
it was just a plumbing
problem. This money devil
smuggles hedgehogs
to the outer reaches
to make its profit. Once
there, the hedgehogs fill
their lairs with grapes
and pears, and curl up
into spiny balls possibly
instinctively, out of fear.
Only a servant of a devil would
scratch its ass with those balls
for pleasure. I sat upon the floor
itching. The other day, a magpie
delivered a mirror to my doorstep.
It carried an image of the deed.
When I heard you'd died
I felt so far away. The magpie cries
out with a cry from a joyless
underworld. It is still the workweek,
I think. "I want to be your friend!"
The magpie cried. Sweet little bird.
You are not primarily
a symbol of death after all!
It folds its wings around itself

and puts its head in a popcorn bag.
I have a poppy in my curly hair.
I carry a purple horn filled
with a soporific drink. What can
I feel anymore that I have not
already felt? How about the ecstatic
states of the Penguin Priests, hopping
up and down with their arms
at their sides, rising up
disappearing into the clouds.
Poof pop poof peck pop poof.
I'm wearing a crocodile on my head
to protect me from the damage
of falling hailstones. I save its
dung to make a salve, so all the evil
in the world will have a nice place
to stay. December is not eternal,
but sometimes it takes a very long
time. The late sun shines through
a skeleton line, dancing around
with trumpets and drums and castanets
trombones, fiddles and majorettes.
Light and shadow and bone.
We dance like the circle
and like the circle the square
is also a very famous shape
for dancing. We'll dance.
We'll dance when we dance
the lower part of our bodies
immovable at first, arms flapping
above us, blown up by a mighty
turbine. Legs break, the sound

of an ox cracking its horns.
And we will do
this all, we'll dance
together something
like that.

Stepping Stone

Faking the voice of summer
in wintertime, I signal
for the southpaw to come in
from the outer snowbank.

I followed the bug down
and once we reach the last basement
stair, The Davy Jones Bug explains
that there are Five Hindrances —
the desire for ordinary
pleasures of sight, sound, and so forth.
Then, "see you later," Davy says
and jumps into the furnace fire.
A green star spinning to
nothing inside a sun.

Outside Paterson

Tell me about your fourth dream?

Pink dawn hitchhiking, I am in a pickup
and I am going to see the doctor
for an annual physical with Jack Nicholson
and he is driving. He's got belly rolls of filet
mignon (sicko!) guzzling spit bug moonshine
foam from a jar. We had never seen each
other before. He says he saw a vision of himself
reborn in a hell world holding a clear monkey
cigar surrounded by nurses and manatees
on fire and came out of that inferno
with an incredible lack of self esteem—germs
he says germs are germs where ever they go
glazed onto the dashboard dark and heavy
lacking dankness and of modest green
a barely satisfactory huff of reefer
from the heating vent whirring hogs
between crustacean shapes but wait
what is in this stuff? Paralyzed chickens,
hospital cinders, a gupping fish maw,
Flossie opening her nightgown
for a locust tree, a red petal edge of sky?
I want to be in a separate examination room,
and away from this drug enforced intimacy.
His hand now is always somewhere on or near
my body. "But since my parents are dead, I could
never get another brother! There is not any
other good doctor within one hundred
and fifty-four miles."

III

The Starfish and the Sea Urchin
Listen to the Sea Cucumber's Song

The light the shine inside
it says the shine inside
the light it says the fire
inside the fire it says the smoke
the air it rings it says the dark
tastes its flesh it says
drawing in the dead light
it says into a throbbing
maw it says the floor
is sand and bones it says
and when the shine is gone
it says it's then the shadows
go it says it's then the
shadows go it says.

Fishy Action

Living free in the wild
little fish all denizens of the deep
bearers of spiritual light
current the darkness
where the sun cannot reach.
All creatures scaly and bare
even the one-eyed fish
scuttle and scrape among
the dazzle rocks. We must always
remember there are some
who by a peculiar twist of mind
seem incapable of appreciating gills
and suckers and fins and the many
amazing facets of fishy action.
Fishy action! They would be so
shocked and delighted when
they finally learn what fishy
action could do for them.
Fishy action! And from then on
they never really let up
talking about it.

Sea Monkeys

Searching, however useless
no water no food—

an abandoned shack
on a little grey hill.

The guidebook warns: the Sun
sets thirteen times faster over

the entire state of Florida.
NOW! permanently on view

underneath the ocean. Nobody
has a golden trident. Nobody

has a golden crown. The people,
the animals, the plants, even

the pastel chalk dust
everything / whatever

moving in all directions
like fireflies used to do.

The sun doesn't like to see
what we have done.

Never Call Them Seagulls

The Gandalf Fishes
feed me their eggs
soft and smooth muscles
cringe and shock the body
growing ovals rolling under
the skin the wink-busted
skulls creak spring crows over
the stubble field's makeshift
meadow everything now
perfectly destitute
radish crammed gills
chain links jagged and torn.
How'd I get to be so biologically
illiterate as to not feel
these colorless birds grow
scarce and disappear?
Why not just kill all
of creation? A return to the moss
garden in the forest snapping
kelp more than I can bear
the foot of a diving duck frozen
in the ditch. You cannot fall
on a pen and die, can you?
The Fish Boat has arrived
—shell the noise through
the dirty shell —this world
will be a night oyster
we can call our own

broken stems on rotten logs
one slip be buried
all manner of flies
are zooming about.

Yonder Bar of Cloud

A ray of light
through it paints

my dead senses red
the crow as strawberry

leather. I am of eternal
simpleton cauliflowers

with leafy edges. How
can it be, how can it be

a secret that we live now
without color. A flower

deep in the center
of The Mountain

its wide petals we
know it piece by piece

the sound of it, the hum
of it, the whole of it

opening is our only
reminder of sun.

Then a Rain That Refreshes
Old Photographs of Rain

Bed before darkness
ran my fingers through you
smoothly modernizing
circuit negativity tables
chemical chargers
an electric fan
dissolves the air
an early orange
cloud insignificant
you know what to say
with a great cry
as if it had been my own
a wooden leg
from my tripod
way up in the sky
without falsehood
spinning away in the wind
nine years pass we now
have sixteen children
papa lord grimy flippers
mama lord sugar doughnuts
probably did it every day
them from you and me
sprays razor sharps
fruit and fat
do not be afraid
we eat them
fruit and fat
this story painting up

its own blue charms
frames with crooked
staples flowers flame up
briefly divine
in this life
half-crazed
a counterfeit
of a heart

    rain cloud
    pale feet
    puff-dust butterfly

I need thee every hour
I need thee every hour.

Blacksmith School Waitlist

From a forge a bit
of metal sang out
orange. I feel
I'm finally in the clear.
Ringing hot nostalgic,
I try to move about
unobserved. But
the iron is no longer
molten once it makes
it to the anvil.
Reminds me
that the time a bee
became my friend
was a great time!
Friend bee somehow
filled the blossoms
with water and took
the nectar at a quickened
pace, the echo of a furry
tongue lapping it up.
I almost didn't
hear it in time.

Isthmus

The Green Sunrise
told to me
the table closest
was the danger
courtyard teetering
snack shack closed
a dark ring pattern
the sign
of The Starfish
the hands
of a dancer turning
from orange
to black
in the fire
at first
with some
shock
The Horse
returned
from The
Whirlwind
"why do you call
that noise a jubilee?"
saffron grasses
sustains breath
moss brawl
the bruised
ball bearings
I was still growing
tried on hoofs

my abandoned
feeling and took
it even deeper inside
prune clothes in tatters
a dark inertia
couldn't get up
but felt exhilarated
across empty headlands
grit clings to me as if
it were the entire
history of grit
closed face eyelids
in the wind
the stinging
tentacles
of The Jellyfish
the fighting
ocean growled
it does not like me
the growl became more
and more noticeable
I don't know
a rolling foam
fish rush into it
play-locks
the spiral sand
belt-stars
around your
waist for about
five minutes
and then
nothing at all.

A Line of Tails

I am BUNNY
among my BUNNY.

I am BUNNY
princess of pancakes.

Raft up a brilliance
of fiery poems so that

the words tangle the mind
a bridge of fire ants

the lonely piano
that made me cry

are transformed
into a swarming.

There's a river
in here somewhere

and I never even
hinted about it

until this very
moment.

Deer Farm Broken

The hill is empty
and that is not a human
voice in my head.

I return to the scene
a year later entering
the deep forest

light on green
moss on repeat
light on green

moss on repeat
light on green
moss on repeat.

The Afternoon Report

The motion of our solar system is slowing,
pulling power from the bodies that still
have love for each other. The earth just rolls
upon itself. What else can it do?
Perhaps there is not a living thing here.
Look up! Do Sun exercises in the Sun.
Moon exercises in the Moon.
Check your eyes by taking hold of the lashes
and pull up slightly to the left. Can you feel
the percolation of water inside? Listen,
it is almost time to drink. Soaked by sudden
cold, you could hear the dripping blood
inside of what is essentially a falling away
of body from spirit here in early autumn
listening to icicles hanging from yak fur.
I forgot what to do with the stars. Why
do you have such a low paying job?
Time crushing breakage is looking
for someone to pay for all this ruin
once we finally have the entire
world to ourselves alone.

Canyon Green

cool mountain caterpillar retreat
bored by all this pupa action
sad: my cricket children
dumb wingless beasts

the moon floats away
turnips then radishes
consecrate to death flies
this swatter empty-handed
bright red blood pepper pod
of a single vine all death popping
shiny mingling with snails
in my newly thatched
a bush murmuring petals

   frog interior hollow
   open your mouth

the evening bell
green orange in my garden
a lovely sunset
fails by its own will

   November uncertain
   stupid storks!

There Is Nothing That Makes
This Winter Garden More Inviting

When the bark slips easily—the middle of the twig is best
glad I could feed them their last sweet drops—it's wet
forgive me it has been a busy day—the vegetable
colors went through all fifty-five green to dead

modulations their basic patterns may evolve around
any triangle—a feeling of wellbeing from attention to doing
something familiar and organized but I avoid
mathematical precision every time with a duck-footed

cultivator—seed pods are silky—papery flesh held in close
roots dug in the fall—pack the grafts in damp sand
—Earthstalk Looper and star Beanleaf Hopper
diamondback larvae hiding in this cabbage

—puffy clouds their edges frayed extended
to the horizon darkening the garden as they spread.

The End of Cheetah Bird

Cheetah Bird your leaves are falling down
and all of your yellow and green spots
and feathers have turned to brown.

Cheetah has changed now.
Cheetah has changed now.

Cheetah wind is playing with the breeze.
It is messing with the breeze.
Oh, Cheetah messing with the breeze,
With its very own wind messing with the breeze.

Cheetah has changed now.
Cheetah has changed now.
It's Cheetah. It's Cheetah.
Cheetah has changed now.
Cheetah has changed now.

It's Cheetah, It's Cheetah.
Cheetah falling down
leaves and wings
leaves and wings
falling to the ground.

Moon Radish

If you can hold a Moon Radish in your hand without looking at it, you will be able to penetrate the subconscious of your Moon Body. Automatically as you interact with this change inside you, you will recognize it first as a white light, then emotion light, provocative light, spiritual light or depth of psychomotor light and so on. You will probably want to recreate this orbiting body state again and again as I have, coming to understand only later how this feeling is the thing we have no choice in, as we sit in the grass watching the field hoppers jump into the sunset, but to believe in consciousnesses between the sub-consciousnesses is to take the whole of the action of holding, of burning, to change its sense without looking, to charge it up, to bring in more colors in order to make the spell ring out—becoming an enormous gong gonging-gonging at the edge of a darkening forest. Now you can hear what I've been longing to see.

What They Said the Way of the Leopards Was

My party drugs need
much larger platters.

After refusing my request
for such several times

the Leopard Lover
the former Lover

of the Leopard's
Lover's Leopard

Lover consented
to my platter desires,

were mine, were Lovers,
were Leopards, were in love

forever and ever like Leopards
can like Leopards do.

The Story of The Leaf

Green energy squirrel tails
cocked up some nut
veins melancholy
loving wooden
creek crack
and shine
to gradually ash the world
your physical
body will reflect
this change nothing
but dark spots
and clouds
in the pictures
the photographs
were a kind
of energy
a counterpart
to the body
of the leaf
the energy body
didn't want
to be a part
of the physical body
anymore
died away
in the distance
a lofty palm
the last sound
of the marauders'
nightly efforts

the rough bamboos
silk pocket fish shoals
in every direction
dipping our heads
back into the water
again over the water
offering to chase us
galaxies sparkling lights
inside our palpitated bodies.
The double is the distinct
belief of the individual.
A capable spiritual
essence—the machine
will never fully explain
to a tree, to a leaf.

Seattle born, C.E. Putnam has lived in four world capitals: London, Singapore, Bangkok, and Washington DC. He currently resides in Portland, Oregon where he operates the Putnam Institute for Space Opera Research. This is his seventh book.